SUMMER

A MENU FOR ALL SEASONS

SUMMER

To Lynne,
Bonne Cuisine!
Pascale Beale

A Montecito Country Kitchen Cookbook

by Pascale Beale-Groom

Foreword by Michel Richard

PUBLISHED BY

Olive Tree Publishing
Santa Barbara, California 93108
PHONE (805) 969-1519
FAX (805) 969-5609

For cooking classes and merchandise:
www.montecitocountrykitchen.com
E-mail: montecitocountrykitchen@cox.net

A Menu For All Seasons 2: Summer
A Montecito Country Kitchen Cookbook
by Pascale Beale-Groom

First Edition

ISBN 0-9749603-2-2
Library of Congress Catalog Number: 2007930560

Design, Digital Production and Printing by Media 27, Inc., Santa Barbara, California

WWW.MEDIA27.COM

Printed and bound in China

Pour Julia

et notre Provence

Menu for the first
days of Summer

Cucumber & Avocado Soup
with a tomato tartare

Summer Vegetable Terrine
with a
Tomato~Lemon Sauce

Caramelized Plums
'Nutty' Meringues

contents

I MET PASCALE in the early 1980s in Los Angeles. She came to Citrus frequently to dine with her family and her future husband, Steven. On a number of occasions she also spent time with us in our kitchen, observing our day-to-day rituals and learning some of the tricks of the trade.

In the twenty years that have passed, she has evolved from a rustic cook to an accomplished cooking school instructor and creator of these delicious recipes with a more refined palate. Her food now reflects the essence of the seasons, and she champions the use of the freshest possible, organic ingredients.

This book captures the tastes and flavors of summer. The Peach and Tomato Salad, and the Cucumber and Avocado Soup, are perfect examples of this. They are simple, flavorful dishes that showcase summer vegetables at their best. The desserts highlight all the succulent summer fruit, the Summer 'Fool' is the perfect dessert for a hot day — cool, sensuous and fresh. The book also reflects the aromas and senses of Mediterranean and Californian cuisines. The Roasted Duck with Olives is just such a dish — a marriage of two cultures, embracing the best of each one.

Pascale also emphasizes a tradition that is close to my heart: that of the family dinner, of taking time to sit with your friends and to enjoy the process of creating a meal together. This is something that is all too often set aside in our busy lives, yet something we should cherish and encourage. The meal doesn't have to be complicated or take a

Michel Richard

8

long time to produce, but rather be an event that pleases everyone, that all can participate in and all can appreciate.

The recipes and text of this 'Summer' book have brought back wonderful memories of the languorous Sunday lunches we used to spend together, enjoying good food, wine and fun with our large, extended family of friends. Lunches that often drifted into dinner, with everyone contributing something to the table. Those days may now be distant memories, but the taste of those meals is long savored.

Pascale's food captures much of that flavor. She has created a cooking school that teaches and promotes this very idea — a place to gather, cook, laugh, taste and enjoy food. Her cookbook is an extension of that principle and the joy of those far off days is represented therein.

This book is clearly set out and beautifully illustrated. The photographs are warm and stimulating. The text has clear timing principles and instructive tips on perfecting dishes. Even more elaborate ones, such as the Summer Terrine, are explained in easy steps, making each succulent layer clear and concise.

From the pleasures of Provence in the guise of the Beignets de Courgettes et d'Aubergines to a taste of the Pacific in the succulent shape of the Cured Salmon with Mesclun Salad, and all the dishes in between, redolent of this hot, vibrant season; this book is the perfect summer feast.

—MICHEL RICHARD

SUMMER is the season that evokes many images for me, usually connected to our home in France — summer meals, barbeques, hot days and picnics, when a chilled paradise cocktail is just the thing. Growing up in London, my brother and I counted the days until the end of school, knowing that we would be rushing off to the South of France. The summer holidays meant the Mediterranean, the sea, the sun, swimming, windsurfing and playing boules under the mulberry trees in the garden or the village square. Most of all summer captured the essence of living in Provence.

Our house was busy with family and friends coming to stay for a few days, and people always coming by for dinner — lots of them. As a teenager, I cooked almost every day throughout the summer, great mounds of food: salads, roasts, fish, pies, onion tarts, summer berries... It proved to be an excellent training ground, with meals held around the large wooden table set on a terra cotta tiled floor in the kitchen/dining room, kept cool in the summer by the three-foot-thick walls of our two-hundred-year old farmhouse. In the middle of August, we held a large *fête* in the garden. A bucolic afternoon, sitting under an Indian canopy that was strung up from the rooftops and attached to the trees, with all the food placed on the well that sits in the middle of the garden. My love of gathering people around a table or well, as the case may be, comes from this time.

I now share these traditions with my own family. Summer is the time to live life a little slower, and as my father would say, 'to take time to smell the roses.' It is a time to savor the flavors of the season, read a book in the hammock, to have a *sieste* during those hot afternoons, build castles and to wiggle your toes in the sand.

Summer is also a time for inventing new dishes and recipe testing. A number of the recipes in this book were created over the five summers my long-time fellow-cook and great friend, Ann Marie (now retired from teaching), and I worked together. I have included many of our favorites, as they capture the essence of the food we created together, including a perennial variation of a long-time signature dish, Pots de Crème.

Other dishes have been developed over the last couple of years, combining new textures and elements of Californian and Provençal cooking, a reflection of the two parts of the world I now call home.

Creating the dishes starts with the raw ingredients. We are spoiled in Provence with an abundance of wonderful markets. Our local one takes place twice a week in what has to be one of the most beautiful town squares in the world. Light filters through centennial plane trees that shade the square. Under their canopy one finds a treasure trove of fresh cheeses, breads, olives and seasonal fruits and vegetables of every kind. Shopping for food is a daily ritual in France and one in which I am a happy and active participant. Inspiration for dishes often comes from meandering in the market and spying something new.

Living in Santa Barbara for most of the year, I come as close as one can come to the delights of the Riviera. Our local farmers' markets offer a plethora of beautiful, fresh, organic produce. The Green and White Summer salad is the result of one such trip, where the ingredients came together in my basket, each one encouraging the addition of another herb or vegetable. I immediately rushed home and chopped them all up. The result was fresh and vibrant — instant gratification on a hot summer's day.

This season is also the busiest in my kitchen as the bulk of the annual batches of jams, chutneys and marmalades are made between June and September. All of this stems from my childhood visits to my grandmother's house in the French Alps. My first task was to pick the fruit in her garden. My grandparents had planted apricot, plum, cherry and apple seedlings when my mother was a child. The full-grown trees produced fragrant, luscious fruit, which were then transformed into all sorts of delights. My two favorites were her Apricot Jam and her Red-Currant Jelly. The first had an amazing flavor — truly the essence of apricots. The second had an extraordinary texture; you felt the fruit pop in your mouth when you ate it. I loved making jam with her and treasured the one jar we could carry back to London with us.

My children are now active participants in this jam-making ritual. They often pick the fruit from our garden and have become quite skilled at stirring the steaming copper cauldrons that hold the fragrant batches. The house is filled with the intense aromas of simmering plums and apricots. It is quite intoxicating.

As Craig Claiborne once said, 'Cooking is at once child's play and adult joy. And cooking done with care is an act of love.' Whatever your summer rituals, I hope that you will take time to enjoy them; take a moment to breath, slowly, and gather your friends around a table, eating fresh, vibrant food.

Pascale

MY GOAL in each of the classes I teach, and, by extension, this book, is to encourage everyone to get together in the kitchen, to have fun preparing a wonderful meal, and to enjoy eating it. Cooking is a structured but creative medium, which draws on and stimulates all senses. Foremost is the creation of the menu. Here is the recipe.

COOK WITH THE SEASONS: Use seasonal fruits and vegetables (organic if possible) in planning your meals. You will taste the difference in your food. The meals you cook will only be as good as the food you buy. 'Old potatoes will taste like old potatoes.'

BEGIN WITH THE HIGHLIGHT OF YOUR MENU: When creating menus I often walk around the local farmers' market for inspiration. There are many dishes that have come about as I have spied some delicious-looking heirloom tomatoes, peaches or berries.

Choosing your main course is often the easiest way to start. Decide if you want to serve fish or meat, poultry or pasta, a vegetarian dish or a hearty salad, for example. This will give you the foundation of the entire meal. Once the key ingredient is chosen, decide if it needs an accompaniment. A stew filled with vegetables probably would not, but a roast chicken would be enhanced by some seasonal vegetables. Don't feel obligated to add potatoes or rice to every dish. Many will stand alone; for example, you could serve the roasted leg of lamb on page 16 with just the roasted tomatoes and snap peas, and it would be delicious.

BALANCE YOUR TASTES AND TEXTURES: Once you have chosen your main course, choose a first course that will complement it. Think of something that will enliven the palate, usually light and enticing, but not so wild that it will jar your tastes. Changes in temperature are also good for your palate. If you serve a very rich soup and then serve a stew, your guests will be overwhelmed. Not only will they be full before you serve your masterpiece but their taste buds will be dulled by the similar nature of each dish's texture. A light fresh citrus salad will open their appetites before a heartier main course. Conversely a small bowl of a savory soup would be wonderful before, say, a grilled fish.

USE DIFFERENT COOKING METHODS: When choosing your dishes bear in mind how they are prepared. If you decide to make a quiche, roast some fish and bake a cake, every item you chose needs to be cooked in the oven, a problem if you only have one oven. Using different cooking methods will ease preparation and will also enhance the differences in textures.

SAVOR WHAT YOU ARE PREPARING: Enjoy pleasing yourself and those you are cooking for. They will taste your enthusiasm in the food.

THE KEY, I have found, to getting the most out of all your culinary efforts is twofold. The first is using the best possible, freshest, seasonal fruits, vegetables and produce available. The second is timing. Proper timing is being able to get the whole meal on the table when you want it, without one dish being half-cooked whilst another is overdone. Many have lamented to me over the past few years that they can roast a chicken but cannot get the vegetables or salads ready at the same time. Others get flustered at the very thought of having more than two people over for a meal. Friends in our home always congregate in the kitchen, for it is truly the heart of the house. I hope that you will have the same traffic jam around your kitchen counters. Give your guests a glass of wine, something to nibble on, and stop worrying.

Every menu in this book emphasizes what I teach in every class: timing is the key to a successful meal. Here, you will find a simple technique to help with timing. You can create your own cooking schedules for any meal you prepare by adhering to the following cooking schedule:

1   Read the recipes two or three times before you start preparing and cooking in order to familiarize yourself with the procedure, the utensils and equipment you will need. This is especially true if you are making a new dish.

2   Gather all the ingredients you need for each dish before you start cooking. This will save time in the preparation.

3   Decide the time at which you wish to eat your MAIN course and write it down on the bottom of a piece of a paper. This will form the basis of your schedule.

4   Working backwards from that time, you will be able to calculate how long you will need to cook your main course. For example, if you are baking fish, you will often find that you are putting the fish in the oven only as you sit down to eat the first course, as fish, in most cases, needs so little time to cook.

5   Write down the time of your first course, allowing for 20 – 30 minutes between your first and main course.

6   Then work out how much time you need to prepare each of your dishes and allocate an order to them, preparing the dish that takes the longest time first. The majority of the time, this seems to be dessert. You will also find out that this means that you may be putting dishes in the oven, finishing sauces and so on, after your guests have arrived. Do not panic and rest assured that if you have prepared the ingredients ahead of time and written down the order in which you are going to cook them, your meal will be a success.

Bearing the above in mind, feel free to mix and match the recipes in the book or cook one dish.

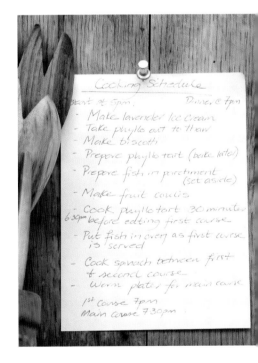

Beignets de Courgettes et d'Aubergines, Sauce Tomates à l'Ail
Roasted Leg of Lamb Stuffed with Black Olive Tapenade
and a Confit of Tomatoes
Summer Sugar Snap Peas
Caramelized Plums with Nutty Meringues

COOKING SCHEDULE

In the morning make the confit of tomatoes — they take 10 minutes to prepare but take 7 hours to cook.

- Make the meringues — they can be made earlier in the day if you like.

Starting 2 hours before you plan to eat your first course:

- Prepare the plums and ingredients and set aside — they will cook as you are eating the main course.

- Prepare the tapenade.

- Prepare the lamb — this will take about 10 – 15 minutes.

1 1/2 hours before you plan to eat your MAIN course, put the lamb in the oven.

- Make the batter for the beignets.

- Prepare the vegetables for the beignets.

- Make the sauce tomates à l'ail.

- Just before sitting down to the first course, cook the beignets — they need to be hot and freshly cooked.

- Remove the lamb from the oven and let it rest for 10 minutes before you slice it.

- Cook the snap peas between the first and main course as they only take a few minutes.

- Place the pan with the plums on the stove as you sit down to eat the main course.

BEIGNETS DE COURGETTES ET D'AUBERGINES
(Zucchini and Eggplant Provençal Fritters)

This Provençal treat comes from the very first class Ann Marie and I taught together. It is the perfect dish to serve with an aperitif on long, languid summer evenings. Served with a salad, it also makes a delicious lunch.

Serves 8 people

For the batter:

3 egg yolks

3 tablespoons olive oil

1 1/3 cups beer

6 oz (1 1/2 cups) unbleached flour

Salt and freshly ground pepper

3 egg whites

1 small bunch regular parsley — stems removed and chopped (about 1/2 cup)

1   With a whisk beat the egg yolks and then very slowly add the oil, beer and flour, beating constantly to prevent lumps. Season with salt and pepper and set aside, covered in a warm place for 1 hour.

For the vegetables:

4 medium courgettes (zucchini) — sliced lengthwise into 1/4-inch strips

2 medium aubergines (eggplant) — sliced into 1/4-inch rounds

Fresh thyme

2 tablespoons olive oil

Salt and pepper

1   Blanch the courgettes and aubergines for 3 minutes in boiling salted water. Drain.

2   Dry all of the vegetables and marinate them in the salt, pepper, olive oil and fresh thyme for 1 hour.

To cook the beignets:

1   Beat the egg whites until stiff but not dry and fold them gently into the batter. Add the parsley and the marinated vegetables.

2   Heat the oil in a large frying pan or a deep fryer. Test the oil by dropping a little batter in it. If it sizzles it is ready to use. Using tongs, pick the vegetables out of the batter shaking off any excess and drop into the oil one at a time. Do not add too many to the oil at once as it will lower the temperature and the beignets will stick together. The beignets should have enough room to roll over easily. Fry them for 4 to 5 minutes until golden brown. Drain them on a layer of paper towels. Place them on a baking tray and cover them with more paper towels. When they are all ready, place them in a basket or a serving dish. Serve as soon as possible, as they will lose their crispness if they wait too long. Serve with the sauce tomates à l'ail (see recipe below).

THE KEY

To make these great beignets you need to let the batter rest for 1 hour before adding the egg whites. Once the whites are added, use the batter immediately. Also make sure that the oil you use is hot enough, otherwise you will have heavy, soggy-tasting fritters. The use of rice and/or corn flour will also make a lighter, crisper batter.

Origins

Beignets is the French word for a type of fritter—a deep-fried choux pastry. These vegetable *beignets* are a traditional dish in the South of France. Many towns in France have their own versions (usually a sweet variety) with a specific shape and their own names. In Montpellier they are known as *merveilles*, *bugnes* in Lyon, *rousettes* in Strasbourg, *tourtisseaux* in Anjou. There is also a small plain version with the rather cheeky name, known as *pet de nonne* ~ nun's fart!

SAUCE TOMATES À L'AIL

Serves 8 people

1 large onion — finely diced

3 lbs. ripe tomatoes — roughly chopped

2 cloves garlic — finely diced

2 tablespoons olive oil

2 tablespoons butter

Fresh thyme

Fresh basil

1   Heat the oil and butter in a heavy-bottomed skillet and add the finely-chopped onions. Cook until translucent and soft, approximately 8 – 10 minutes, over medium-low heat. Add the garlic and cook for 1 minute more.

2   Add the tomatoes, stirring vigorously and cook until the bulk of the liquid has evaporated, creating a thick sauce. Stir in the fresh thyme and cook for 3 more minutes.

3   Stir in the basil and serve immediately.

Stuffing and tying the leg of lamb

ROASTED LEG OF LAMB STUFFED WITH BLACK OLIVE TAPENADE AND A CONFIT OF TOMATOES

Gigot d'agneau (leg of lamb) is a very traditional dish in the South of France, usually made with garlic and some fresh herbs, such as rosemary and thyme. This version is a little more exotic. The heavenly tomatoes bring an added richness and depth of taste to the dish. It is also beautiful when sliced as the stuffing creates a wonderful pattern inside the roast.

Serves 10 – 14 people

1 whole leg of lamb, approximately 4 1/2 lbs boned — trimmed of all fat and butterflied but not tied. Ask your butcher to butterfly the lamb for you.

Olive oil

6 tablespoons black olive tapenade (recipe follows)

24 *tomates confites* (recipe follows)

8 – 10 garlic cloves — peeled

Coarsely ground black pepper

Sea salt

Herbes de Provence

10 – 12 roma tomatoes — quartered

1 1/2 cups red wine for deglazing the roasting pan

2 cups chicken stock for basting

1   Preheat the oven to 425 degrees.

2   Place the lamb on a chopping board, opening it up so that it lies flat, cut side up. It will look like an elongated S. Spoon the black olive tapenade onto the length of the lamb, spreading it evenly over the meat. Lay the *tomates confites* down the center of the roast, on top of the tapenade. Fold the lamb back to its original shape now containing the tapenade and confits in the middle of the roast.

3   Using kitchen string, tie the leg of lamb at evenly spaced intervals. Once tied, cover the outside of the roast with olive oil. Make small slits into the meat and push in the remaining garlic cloves. Cover the roast with Herbes de Provence and some black pepper and sea salt. Place the lamb in a roasting dish. Surround the lamb with the roma tomatoes. Drizzle a little olive oil on the tomatoes.

4   Bake the lamb at 425 degrees for 15 minutes, and then lower the temperature to 400 degrees. At this point add a little water or chicken stock to the baking dish — just half way up the sides of the tomatoes — approximately 1 1/4 cups.

5 Continue to roast the lamb for an additional 1 hour and 10 minutes — 1 hour and 20 minutes depending on the size and how pink you like your meat.

6 Once cooked, remove the lamb from the oven, place it on a chopping board, cover loosely with foil and let it rest for 10 – 15 minutes. While it is resting make the sauce.

7 Place the roasting dish on the stove top. Pour the red wine into the pan, scraping up all the bits as you go. Bring the wine to a rapid boil and let it reduce by 3/4. Add the remaining chicken stock to the sauce and reduce it a little more.

Taste for seasoning, adding salt and pepper to your liking. Add one or two teaspoons of butter to give the sauce a nice sheen.

8 Thinly slice the lamb and serve on warm plates with some of the sauce, tomatoes and snap peas.

This menu is a great showcase of summer's best vegetables and fruits. It may take a little longer to prepare, but it is well worth the effort. It is perfect for a summer's eve dinner party and everyone will enjoy the beautiful plums with their nutty meringue accompaniment.

BLACK OLIVE TAPENADE

This will make enough for one leg of lamb with a little left over — perfect on toast for the cooks as they work in the kitchen!

10 oz (1 cup) black Nicoises olives — pitted

Juice of 1 lemon and the grated zest of the same lemon

1/3 cup olive oil

6 anchovy filets, cleaned, rinsed and drained

2 teaspoons capers

Freshly ground pepper

1   Place all the olives, half of the lemon juice, the lemon zest, olive oil, anchovies, capers and some ground pepper in a small food processor or a mortar and pestle.

2   Process or grind the olives until they form a coarse paste, using more lemon juice if the mixture is too dry. Set aside.

CONFIT OF TOMATOES

12 Medium round tomatoes — cut in half

Olive oil

1   Place the tomatoes, cut side up on a baking sheet. Drizzle with a little olive oil and bake in a 250 degree oven for 7 hours. That is not a typo! You can do this the day before and keep them packed in a little olive oil in a covered bowl overnight. They can also be kept in a jar completely covered with olive oil for up to a week. Be sure the tomatoes are totally submerged otherwise they will go bad.

THE KEY:

Do not rush these tomatoes. For the first two hours it seems as if not much has happened. Resist the temptation to turn up the oven. The long cooking time concentrates the tomato flavor so that they resemble soft sun-dried tomatoes. It is well worth your time.

SUMMER SUGAR SNAP PEAS

1 1/2 lbs sugar snap peas

1 tablespoon olive oil

1 oz (2 tablespoons) butter

Salt and pepper

Freshly chopped chives

1   Melt the butter and olive oil in a large skillet, over medium heat. Add the peas and cook for 3 –4 minutes, adding the salt, pepper and chives just at the end, tossing well. Serve hot.

CARAMELIZED PLUMS

Serves 8 people

3 oz (6 tablespoons) butter

1 tablespoon light brown sugar

1 tablespoon honey

1 teaspoon cinnamon

1 1/2 lbs ripe plums —
   quartered and pitted —
   use different varieties if possible

1 tablespoon sliced Marcona almonds

1   Melt the butter in a large skillet placed over medium-high heat. Once the butter is foaming, add in the light brown sugar, honey and cinnamon. Cook for 2 – 3 minutes and then add in the plums. Cook for 10 – 12 minutes over low heat so that the plums are lightly golden.

2   Just before serving, sprinkle the plums with the almonds. Spoon the plums onto dessert plates, being sure to spoon some of the delicious syrup that will have formed in the bottom of the pan. Serve the meringues alongside.

NOTE: This is also wonderful with a dollop of freshly-whipped cream or vanilla ice cream.

NUTTY MERINGUES

Serves 8 – 10 people

3 egg whites

7 1/2 oz sugar —
    (1 cup less 2 level tablespoons)

2 tablespoons finely chopped assorted
    nuts (pecans, pistachios and
    macadamias make a great mix)

1　Preheat the oven to 225 degrees.

2　Place the egg whites in a mixing
bowl and beat until they hold soft peaks.
Gradually add the sugar, a tablespoon
at a time and whisk until the whites are
stiff and very glossy. Add in the chopped
nuts and beat a few seconds more so
that they are evenly distributed in the
meringue mixture.

3　Drop large tablespoonfuls of the
mixture onto a parchment-lined baking
sheet. Bake in the oven for one hour
and 30 minutes or until they are dry
and crisp. They should not turn golden,
but rather should be a pale cream color
when finished. You can also pipe the
meringue mixture using a normal round
nozzle attachment to create evenly
shaped meringues.

THE KEY:

*When making meringues, always beat
the egg whites first before slowly adding
the sugar, otherwise you will have flat
meringues which fail to hold their shape.*

Origins

Meringues originated in 17th century Europe. The first printed record of
them appears in Massialot in 1691. For a time they had the charming name
of *sugar puffs* before the word meringue came into regular use. Chefs used to
use a whisk made of birch twigs to beat the egg whites before the invention
of more conventional utensils. Marie-Antoine Carême, the world-renowned
19th century French chef, was the first to use a piping bag to form the
meringue into different shapes.

Green & White Summer Salad

Marmalade Salmon with Wedding Rice

Raspberry Ginger Pots de Crème

COOKING SCHEDULE

Starting 2 hours before you plan to eat your first course:

- Make the raspberry ginger pots de crème.

- Prepare step 1 of the Wedding Rice.

- Prepare the salmon, but do not cook until ready to sit down for the first course.

- Finish the rice.

- Prepare the summer salad and toss just before you serve.

- Put salmon in oven just as you sit down to eat the first course.

GREEN & WHITE SUMMER SALAD

Serves 8 people

Olive oil

Zest of 1 lemon

1 lb snap peas

1 lb English peas — shelled

1 English cucumber — diced

4 stems green onions — thinly sliced

1 Granny Smith apple — cored and diced

1/3 cup fresh mint leaves — thinly sliced

1/4 cup fresh dill — chopped

4-inch long piece daikon radish — diced

6 oz feta — crumbled

Freshly ground pepper

Lemon juice of 1 lemon

2 tablespoons tarragon vinegar

1   Pour a little olive oil into a large pan placed over medium heat. Add in the lemon zest, a good pinch of salt, snap peas and English peas and sauté for 5 minutes. Whilst they are cooking, prepare the rest of the salad.

2   Place the cucumber, green onions, apple, radish, mint, feta and dill in a salad bowl. Add the lemon juice, a drizzle of olive oil and tarragon vinegar over the top. Add the cooked English peas to the salad bowl and toss gently so that all the ingredients are evenly distributed.

NOTE: This is excellent served with warm olive bread.

Origins

Marmalade has a long history. It has also changed its consistency over the centuries from a firm, sweet, quince-like paste exported to England by the Portuguese in the 15th century, called *Marmalada*, to the more liquid version we are familiar with today. This version, it is believed, has its origins in Scotland. There are numerous recipes in 16th and 17th century cookbooks that refer to a clear type of this *marmalada*, then called *quiddony* in England and *cotignac* in France, which was thick and cut into slices. The addition of more water to liquefy the mixture appears in recipe books a century or so later. There are now thousands of types of marmalades, usually all containing the peel of the fruit.

❦

MARMALADE SALMON

We had just made 100 pounds of marmalade for the cooking school. I usually make desserts with it, but Ann Marie created this beautiful, simple, savory dish with it. The marmalade is the perfect foil for the salmon. This is a great dish for a party too, as it can be eaten cold.

Serves 8 people

3 lbs salmon filet — skin left on

6 oz marmalade or enough to cover the salmon

1 This dish can be prepared either in the oven or grilled. The cooking technique is the same.

2 If cooking in the oven, place the salmon filet in a shallow roasting pan or on a baking sheet. Spoon the marmalade all over the salmon. If grilling on the barbecue, prepare the salmon in the same manner, putting it on foil so that you can easily transfer it to the grill.

3 Cook the salmon under the broiler for 8 – 10 minutes. If grilling, cover the salmon lightly with a foil tent and cook for 8 – 10 minutes.

4 Serve on warm plates with the Wedding Rice.

WEDDING RICE

In celebration of our lovely friends Tricia and Michael's nuptials, Ann Marie and I created their wedding feast. Cooking under the trees in their garden, we made this Kurdish inspired dish. We named it Wedding Rice in honor of the beautiful day we shared together.

Serves 8 people

3 onions medium-sized thinly sliced

2 garlic cloves — crushed

1 tablespoon ground cumin

1 tablespoon ground cinnamon

1 teaspoon ground nutmeg

1 tablespoon curry powder

1/2 cup pine nuts

1/2 cup almonds — sliced and roasted

1/2 cup golden raisins

2 cups basmati rice — rinsed

3 cups chicken stock

1 Pour a little olive oil in a large heavy-bottomed skillet placed over medium heat and sauté the onions, garlic and spices until the onions are soft — about 8 – 10 minutes. Add the pine nuts, almonds and raisins and cook a minute or two more.

2 Pour the chicken stock and rice into a rice cooker and then stir the onion mixture into the rice. Cover and cook. If you do not have a rice cooker you can do this in a large saucepan. The rice will take 15 – 20 minutes to cook. Be careful not to let it burn! Keep the lid on the rice, as this will keep it warm, but remove the pan from the heat after it is cooked.

RASPBERRY GINGER POTS DE CRÈME

In every cooking series we taught together, Ann Marie and I had a new pots de crème recipe. I have developed a fondness for these delicious creamy desserts that borders on fanaticism. This is my favorite summer version, combining delicate raspberries with the tang of fresh and crystallized ginger.

Serves 8 people

2 1/2 cups cream

5 oz (1/2 cup plus 2 tablespoons) super fine sugar

A small 1/2 inch piece of fresh ginger — peeled and grated

1/3 cup lemon juice

1 oz crystallized ginger — finely chopped

1/2 cup fresh raspberries

1   Place the cream, sugar and fresh ginger in a small saucepan and stir constantly over medium heat until the mixture boils. Reduce heat and simmer for 5 minutes. Remove from the heat, add the lemon juice and crystallized ginger and let stand for 5 minutes.

2   Carefully add in the raspberries and fold in gently to combine.

3   Divide the mixture evenly amongst eight small cups or ramekins, cover and refrigerate for at least 2 hours or until the mixture has set.

THE KEY:

For a pot de crème to set successfully you need to let the cream and sugar boil and then simmer. This will allow all the sugar to melt properly. If you shorten the time the cream cooks, it will not set correctly. Adding the lemon juice at this point will ensure that the mixture thickens.

Origins

Raspberries have been around since prehistoric times. They were originally cultivated by the ancient Greeks and were highly regarded for their delicate flavor. Although not widely-cultivated until the 20th century, there are accounts of raspberries for culinary purposes in the writings of Pliny the Elder in the 1st century AD. They can vary in color from almost black to white,

Peach and Heirloom Tomato Salad

Roasted Duck with Olives and Herb Couscous

Poached Summer Fruit with Citrus Cookies

COOKING SCHEDULE

Starting 2 hours before you plan to eat your first course:

- Make the Citrus Cookies.

- Prepare the fruit and poach them — this can be made a few hours in advance if you like.

- Prepare and cook the duck with olives.

- Prepare the ingredients for the salad. Assemble no more than one hour before serving.

- Prepare the ingredients for the herb couscous but do not cook until just before you sit down for the first course as it only takes 20 minutes to cook.

PEACH AND HEIRLOOM TOMATO SALAD

I had a very large yellow and red heirloom tomato in my kitchen and had just picked some peaches which were remarkably similar in size and color. I sliced through both fruit, drizzled fig purée over the top and added some pink sea salt. The peach and tomato juices married so well together and the taste was fresh and succulent. It is one of my favorite summer salads.

Serves 8 people

4 large heirloom tomatoes of different varieties

4 large yellow peaches

3 sprigs basil — leaves thinly sliced

4 oz goat cheese

Freshly-ground black pepper

Coarse sea salt

Fig purée (see suppliers list)

1   Using a serrated knife, thinly slice the peaches and the tomatoes. Place all the slices on a large serving dish alternating between the tomatoes and the peaches and creating a circular pattern.

2   Crumble the goat cheese all over the top of the tomatoes and peaches and add the thinly sliced basil leaves. Add freshly ground pepper and a good pinch of the sea salt.

3   Just before serving, drizzle the fig purée over the salad.

THE KEY:

It is most important that you use ripe heirloom tomatoes and ripe peaches. The flavors of the peach and tomato marry perfectly together when the fruits are ripe.

Origins

Heirloom tomatoes are open-pollinated types of tomatoes and generally classified as plants whose origins are at least 50 years old. Their flavor is much richer than conventionally-grown varieties. Some cultivars such as *Brandywine* (from the 1880s) are now becoming more readily available through seed catalogues and farmers' markets.

ROASTED DUCK WITH OLIVES AND HERB COUSCOUS

There is a man in the marché in St. Tropez who only sells olives. He has at least 15 different varieties, prepared in a myriad of ways. Picholine, Nicoises, Greques, Provençal with Herbes de Provence, with garlic, with spices and so on. I have tried them all. There is also a local farmer who brings fresh chickens, poussins, ducks and rabbits to the market. I could not resist the temptation of sautéed rabbit with olives. However as rabbit dishes tend to be a difficult 'sell' in class — much to my chagrin — I created the duck version which is equally delicious. But I have given the rabbit version too, for those of you who wish to try it!

Serves 8 people

8 duck breasts — fat side scored
   with a knife

Olive oil

2 yellow onions — peeled and
   thinly sliced

1 pint black olives — pitted

Salt and pepper

1   Preheat the oven to 400 degrees.

2   Pour a little olive oil in a large pan over medium heat. Add the sliced onions and pitted olives and cook until golden brown — about 8 – 10 minutes.

3   Whilst the onions are cooking, place the duck legs onto a baking sheet or oven-proof dish. Turn the oven to broil and cook the duck legs for 5 – 6 minutes so that they are golden brown. Remove the pan from the oven and add the olive mixture to the duck legs, distributing the olives evenly in the dish. Turn the oven setting back to bake and continue to cook for 25 minutes. Serve on warm plates with the couscous.

The Rabbit Version

If you are preparing the rabbit version you will need 2 rabbits, cut up into eight pieces each to serve eight people. As rabbit is very lean, some of the pieces do not have much meat on them. This version is not cooked in the oven.

1   Prepare the onions as in step 2 of the duck recipe. Remove from the pan and set aside. Pour a little olive oil into the same pan, placed over medium-high heat and add in the rabbit pieces, and a good sprinkling of salt and pepper. Sauté the pieces until they are golden brown on all sides. This will take 10 minutes.

2   Add in 2 cups of rich chicken stock and the onion/olive mixture and bring to a strong simmer. Combine the ingredients well, reduce to a gentle simmer, cover and cook for 30 minutes. Check the pieces from time to time, turning them occasionally. Serve on warm plates with the couscous.

Origins

Olives have been cultivated in the Mediterranean basin for more than 10,000 years. Olive oil played an important culinary and medicinal role in Greek and Roman history and its use spread throughout Europe in pre-biblical times. Thousand-year-old presses have been found in Italy, Israel and all over the Middle East, some of which are still in use today. Spain, now the world's largest producer of olive oil, is responsible for introducing the fruit to the Americas. The beautiful sage-green trees are slow-growing and long-lived. There are trees near our house in Provence that are over 1,000 years old.

HERB COUSCOUS

Serves 8 people

For the couscous:

1 1/2 cups water

1 tablespoon olive oil

1 1/2 cups dry couscous

1/2 teaspoon coarse salt

For the herbs:

1 bunch flat leaf parsley —
finely chopped

1 bunch chives — finely chopped

3 sprigs thyme — stems removed
and leaves chopped

1/4 cup olive oil

1/4 cup lemon juice

Large pinch coarse grey sea salt

Freshly ground pepper

1 Bring the water to a boil with the salt and olive oil in a saucepan. Once the water has boiled, add the couscous, stir to combine, remove from the heat, cover with a lid, and let stand for 5 – 7 minutes. Let the couscous cool slightly and then fluff with a fork.

2 Place all of the ingredients for the herbs, including the lemon juice and olive oil in a medium-sized serving bowl and stir to combine. Add in the warm couscous and stir so that the herbs are well distributed. The couscous should look quite green.

Origins

Centuries old, couscous is a staple in Algeria, Tunisia and Morocco. It is made from hard wheat semolina and resembles tiny balls. Couscous, or *Kuskusu* in Arabic, means well-rolled or rounded. It is also the name of the national dish of Algeria where it is traditionally served after the *Mechoui* — grilled meats, along with chick peas and other vegetables. In Morocco it often follows Tajines and is served with spicy poultry or meat stews.

POACHED SUMMER FRUIT

Serves 8 people

1 cup water

3/4 cup sugar

1/2 cup sweet dessert wine —
   a Montbazilliac or Sauternes

8 – 10 apricots — quartered

4 – 6 peaches — quartered

1 pinch cinnamon

1 pinch nutmeg

Fresh berries of your choice

Fresh mint leaves

1   Place the water, sugar and wine in a medium-sized saucepan over medium-high heat. Cook until the mixture thickens, the sugar has completely dissolved and resembles a light syrup. This will take 7 – 10 minutes.

2   Add the apricots and peaches to the mixture with the cinnamon and nutmeg and cook for 5 minutes. Remove from the heat and let the fruit cool in the poaching liquid.

3   Divide the poached fruit amongst dessert bowls and then spoon some of the fresh berries on top. Place one or two mint leaves and serve with the citrus cookies.

CITRUS COOKIES

Makes 30 cookies

6 oz (1 1/2 sticks) butter

2 teaspoons lemon olive oil

4 oz (just under 1/2 cup) sugar

Zest of 1 large orange (you can use
   blood oranges when in season)

1/2 teaspoon freshly ground pepper

10 oz (2 1/4 cups) flour

1 tablespoon orange juice

1   Preheat the oven to 300 degrees.

2   Place the butter in a standing mixer fitted with a paddle attachment. Beat on medium speed until soft and fluffy. Add in the lemon olive oil and sugar, and beat again until well combined, scraping down the sides of the mixing bowl occasionally.

3   Add in the orange zest, juice, pepper and half the flour and mix together at slow speed. Add in the remaining flour and mix again until the dough has just come together. Remove the dough from the bowl and combine into a ball.

4   Lightly flour a counter top or clean work surface and place the dough in the center. Gently roll out the dough until it is approximately 1/4-inch thick. Using a round, fluted cookie cutter, cut out the cookies and then place them on a parchment-lined baking sheet.

5   Cook the cookies for 45 minutes in the center of the oven. They should be a pale golden color. Place them on a wire rack to cool. They will keep for several days in a sealed container.

Pascale's daughter, Olivia, shopping for peaches.

Phyllo Tart with Tomatoes, Goat Cheese and Dill
Sea Bass Baked in Parchment Paper with Tomato and Black Olive Tapenade
Wilted Garlic Spinach
Lavender Ice Cream, Multi-Berry Coulis and Lemon Biscotti

COOKING SCHEDULE

*Prepare the ice cream — you
can do this earlier in the day or
even the day before.*

- Make the biscotti — this can
  also be made the day before.

- Thaw the phyllo either in the
  refrigerator for 24 hours or
  at room temperature for 4
  hours.

*Starting 2 hours before you plan
to eat your first course:*

- Prepare the phyllo tart but
  do not bake it.

- Prepare the parchment-
  baked sea bass but do not
  bake.

- Make the multi-berry coulis
  and refrigerate.

- Bake the phyllo tart 30
  minutes before sitting down
  to eat the first course.

- Place the fish in the oven
  as you sit down to eat the
  first course (allowing 15 – 20
  minutes to cook the fish).

- Cook the spinach between
  the first and main courses.

PHYLLO TART WITH TOMATOES, GOAT CHEESE AND DILL

*The field next to our farmhouse in the South of France used to have so
many tomatoes that they would be left on the ground to rot by the owners.
We would occasionally rescue the tomatoes from otherwise fertilizing the
soil. Between the tomatoes and the fabulously fresh goat cheese available
at the local farmers' market, numerous variations and dishes were created
including this one, after I found a good local source for the phyllo dough.
It also makes a perfect lunchtime main course when served with a salad.*

Serves 8 people

1 package phyllo dough — thawed
   at room temperature for at least 4
   hours — see instructions on package

7–8 medium tomatoes of any variety —
   but Roma or heirloom are particularly
   good — thinly sliced

1 bunch fresh dill — finely chopped

10 oz log plain goat cheese — crumbled

4 oz (1 stick) butter —
   melted in a small saucepan

Black pepper

Black olives

Olive oil

1   Preheat oven to 400 degrees.

2   On a large clean work surface, lay
out the phyllo dough. Cut the phyllo into
a large square by trimming the end off
the dough. Cover it with a sheet of plastic
wrap and a damp cloth. The square
should be larger than the tart pan (use a
pan with a removable bottom). Take one
sheet of the phyllo dough and lay it on
the tart pan, fitting into the shape of the
pan. Lightly brush the dough with some
of the melted butter. Sprinkle the dough
with a sixth of the dill.

3   Lay another sheet of the phyllo
dough on top of the one already in the
pan, but at a slight angle to the previous
sheet. This will cause the squares to be
offset. Lightly brush the dough with
some of the melted butter. Sprinkle the
dough with a sixth of the dill.

4   Repeat step 3, three more times each
time off-setting the dough a little.

5   Fill the bottom of the phyllo tart
with the crumbled goat cheese.

6   Cover the goat cheese with the
tomatoes starting from the outside edge
of the tart working inwards in concentric
circles of slightly overlapping tomatoes.
Sprinkle the tomatoes with the
remaining chopped dill, the olives and
drizzle a little olive oil over the tomatoes.
Add some black ground pepper.

7   Bake in the oven for 25 minutes. The
edges will be golden brown, the dough
crispy and the tomatoes slightly roasted.

THE KEY:

*The trick with phyllo dough is to work
quickly and not let the dough dry
out — hence the damp cloth. Make
sure you cover the dough each time
you remove a sheet.*

Origins

Phyllo or Filo is the Greek name (meaning leaf) for this paper-thin dough used to make Baklava and Spanokopita. It is made with flour and water. This type of dough originated in Turkey where records of a pleated type of bread occur as early as the 11th century. Phyllo is not created by folding and refolding a sheet of dough as with puff pastry, but by stretching a single sheet until it is almost paper-thin. The layering effect comes from stacking sheet upon sheet with butter brushed between the layers. Since it is extremely labor intensive to make, most people buy pre-made phyllo today.

SEA BASS BAKED IN PARCHMENT PAPER WITH TOMATO AND BLACK OLIVE TAPENADE

The flavors of the French and Italian Riviera are captured in the preparation of this fish and perfect for all the beautiful tomatoes that are available at this time of year. The dish is succulent and bursting with flavor.

Serves 6 – 8 people

2 lbs Sea Bass (cut into 4 oz filets)

10 oz (1 cup) black Nicoises olives — pitted, plus 5 oz (1/2 cup) olives unpitted

Juice and zest of 1 lemon

1/3 cup olive oil

1 lb mixed tomatoes — (yellow, red, heirloom, pear etc. — the choice is yours — they can all be Roma but a little variety adds extra depth to the sauce) roughly chopped

2 large red onions — diced

2 large yellow onions — diced

1/2 cup white wine

Coarse sea salt and pepper

1   Heat oven to 400 degrees.

2   Prepare black olive tapenade. Place all the olives, half the lemon juice, all the lemon zest, the olive oil and a pinch of salt and some ground pepper in a small food processor or a mortar and pestle.

3   Process or grind the olives until they form a coarse paste. Set aside.

4   In a saucepan heat a little olive oil and add the red and yellow onion. Cook over medium heat for 5 – 7 minutes to soften them. Add the tomatoes and cook for 2 – 3 minutes more. Set aside.

5   Cut a piece of parchment paper or foil to about three times the size of the filet. Spoon a large tablespoon of the tomato mixture into the middle of the parchment paper. Place the filet on top of the tomatoes. Spread some of the tapenade all over the top of the filet.

Drizzle a little white wine and lemon juice over the fish and add 2 or 3 olives to the package. Seal the packages by crimping the paper together. Repeat with the remaining filets. Place the finished packages in a baking pan.

6   Bake the fish for 15 – 20 minutes depending on the thickness of the filets — allowing 10 minutes per inch.

7   To serve, open the packages and using a spatula remove the fish with the onions and tomatoes. Carefully pour the cooking juices around and over the fish.

WILTED GARLIC SPINACH

1 lb baby spinach — washed and trimmed of any large stalks

5 – 6 cloves of garlic

Olive oil

1 teaspoon butter

Pepper

1   Preheat the oven to 375 degrees.

2   Place the garlic cloves unpeeled in some foil and wrap them up. Bake in the oven for 45 minutes. Remove from the foil pouch once cooked and squeeze out the soft garlic. Set aside.

3   Just before serving your spinach dish, heat a little olive oil and add the butter to a large frying pan or wok placed over medium-high heat. Add the cooked garlic and then the spinach. Cook very briefly, the leaves should be wilted. Add some pepper to taste.

Origins

Lavender is thousands of years old. It was used by the Phoenicians and Egyptians in mummification and perfumes. The Romans are responsible for its spread throughout both Europe and England as they used it widely in their baths and for medicinal purposes. The word lavender comes from these times as *lavare* means to wash or from *livendula* which means bluish.

Queen Elizabeth I was said to enjoy relishes and condiments perfumed with lavender. France is now the world's largest producer of lavender, exporting 1,000 tons of essential oil a year. It takes a staggering 80 lbs of lavender to make one ounce of oil!

LAVENDER ICE CREAM

During the time we taught together, Ann Marie became the ice cream diva. Our mutual passion for lavender perfumed many of the dishes we created together, and this one is no exception. It found its way into recipes for beef, pots de crème and now this ice cream, which is just the way ice cream should be, a little decadent.

Serves 6 – 8 people

2 tablespoons lavender flowers — finely chopped

2 tablespoons Muscat wine or other white dessert wine

2 1/2 cups heavy cream

7 tablespoons lavender sugar (see recipe below)

2 egg whites

1 Stir the lavender flowers in the dessert wine and leave to infuse for 10 minutes.

2 Beat the cream until stiff but still glossy then gradually mix in the strained wine (reserve the lavender flowers) and half the sugar.

3 Beat the egg whites until stiff, and then beat in the remaining sugar. Fold the egg whites into the cream with the reserved lavender flowers.

4 Spoon the mixture into a bowl and freeze. (In a shallow bowl the ice cream takes 3 – 4 hours to freeze) It will keep covered in the freezer for 5 – 6 days.

For the lavender sugar:

8 oz sugar

4 sprigs lavender

1 Place the sugar and lavender sprigs (in their entirety) in a jar and let sit for a few days. The lavender will perfume the sugar. You may have to stir the sugar from time to time to prevent it from clumping.

MULTI-BERRY COULIS

Serves 8 people

1 lb summer berries, such as raspberries, strawberries, blackberries, etc. Avoid too many dark fruit such as blueberries as they will make the coulis very dark.

2 tablespoons Grand Marnier or Chambord (optional)

1 In a food processor purée the berries.

2 Pour the purée into a bowl and stir in the Grand Marnier. Keep refrigerated until ready to serve. If you want to have a very smooth coulis, strain the purée through a sieve before adding the Grand Marnier, then proceed in the same manner.

LEMON BISCOTTI

Makes 30 medium-sized cookies

4 oz (1 cup) almond meal or almond flour

1/4 cup almonds — roughly chopped

9 oz (2 cups) flour

1 1/2 teaspoons baking powder

1/4 teaspoon salt

3 eggs beaten

3 1/2 oz (1/2 cup) sugar

1/2 teaspoon pure lemon extract

Zest of 2 lemons

1   Preheat the oven to 350 degrees.

2   In a large mixing bowl, using a whisk, combine the eggs, sugar, lemon extract and lemon zest. Mix well and set aside.

3   In a separate bowl combine the flour, almond meal, chopped almonds, baking powder and salt and then gradually add to the egg mixture until combined. The dough will be sticky.

4   On a lightly-floured surface, form the dough into a 3-inch wide by 16-inch long log. Place the log in the center of a parchment-lined baking sheet and flatten it slightly with the palm of your hand. Bake 25 minutes. The log should be golden in color. Remove from the oven and cool on a rack for 5 minutes or until cool enough for you to handle.

5   Cut the log into 1/2-inch wide slices with a serrated knife. Lay the slices on their sides on the baking sheet and bake for 5 minutes. Turn over the Biscotti and then bake on the other side for 5 minutes more. Be careful not to over bake. They will harden when they cool on a wire rack. Store in an airtight container.

Origins

These traditional Italian cookies have been baked for centuries and have been found in early recipe books from the 17th century. They were praised by sailors, soldiers and travelers as they could be stored for a long time. The word biscotti comes from the Middle French word *bescuit,* now *biscuit,* which means a twice-baked cookie. Many countries and cultures in Europe have these types of cookies — German *Zwiebeck,* English *Rusks,* Jewish *Mandlebroit.*

Field Greens and Fennel Salad with Roquefort and Grapes
with a Warm Candied Shallot Vinaigrette

Marinated Grilled Beef with Grilled Vegetables
and Herb Mayonnaise

Summer 'Fool' with Mint Cream

COOKING SCHEDULE

Starting 2 hours before you plan to eat your first course:

- Prepare all the ingredients for the Fool and refrigerate.

- Prepare the grilled beef marinade 1 hour prior to assembling the skewers.

- Make the herb mayonnaise and then refrigerate.

- Assemble all the beef and vegetable skewers.

- Prepare the shallots for the salad.

- Combine the rest of the salad ingredients; add warm vinaigrette just before serving.

- Light the grill 30 minutes before cooking the beef.

- Cook the beef and tomatoes between the first and main courses.

- Place fruit pouch on grill after serving the main course.

- Assemble the Fool.

FIELD GREENS AND FENNEL SALAD WITH ROQUEFORT AND GRAPES WITH A WARM CANDIED SHALLOT VINAIGRETTE

There is a stall at the Santa Barbara Farmers' Market on Saturday morning that is run by a charming man from Laos. He always has a great variety of bok choy, daikon radishes, long beans and other vegetables that form part of the culinary traditions of Thai, Laotian and Indonesian cooking. He also has a wonderful and abundant variety of herbs including great big bunches of purple basil, beautiful both in color and fragrance. This salad was created with some of his great ingredients. It is a mixture of sweet, sour and salty — a mixture of Southeast Asia and Provence.

Serves 8 people

For the shallots:

8 whole shallots — peeled and cut in half

1 teaspoon butter

1 tablespoon olive oil

2 teaspoons sugar

Salt and pepper

1   Pour the oil and add the butter to a small saucepan or skillet placed over medium-high heat. When the butter has melted, add in the shallots and cook for 10 minutes, turning the shallots occasionally. Reduce the heat to low after 10 minutes and add in the sugar, some salt and pepper and toss the shallots well. Continue cooking the shallots for another 30 – 40 minutes until they become golden brown, glossy and candied. Keep warm until ready to serve.

For the salad:

3/4 lb field greens — washed and dried

1 fennel bulb — sliced and then cut into thin pieces

4 oz Roquefort cheese — crumbled

1/2 lb white grapes — each grape cut in half if they are very big

8 ripe figs — quartered

1 bunch purple basil — thinly sliced

1   Place all the ingredients into a large salad bowl. Pour the warm vinaigrette over the ingredients and toss gently.

For the vinaigrette:

1/4 cup olive oil

2 tablespoons apple bouquet vinegar (see suppliers) or other sweet vinegar

1 teaspoon fig purée (see suppliers)

A pinch of coarse salt

1   In a small bowl combine all the ingredients and whisk together. Pour the vinaigrette into the pan with the shallots, whisking it together with any of the pan juices. Pour the warmed vinaigrette, along with the shallots into the salad bowl and toss well to combine, making sure that when you serve the salad, everyone gets a least 2 pieces of the shallots.

MARINATED GRILLED BEEF WITH GRILLED VEGETABLES AND HERB MAYONNAISE

This is a delicious way of preparing beef for a grill. A lot of the preparation can be done in advance and the recipe multiplies easily if you are serving a large crowd. It's perfect for a summer party in the garden.

Serves 8 people

For the beef:

1/4 cup olive oil

8 – 10 stems (1/4 cup) fresh oregano — chopped

10 – 12 stems (1/4 cup) fresh thyme — chopped

Freshly ground pepper

Coarse salt

2 lbs rib eye beef — cut into 1-inch cubes

1   Soak 16 bamboo skewers in water for a minimum of 30 minutes.

2   In a small mixing bowl, combine all the ingredients except the beef so that it creates a thick marinade. Add in the cubed beef and toss to coat well. Leave to marinate for 1 hour.

3   Whilst the meat is marinating, prepare the onions and the courgettes (zucchini). See below.

4   Assemble the skewers in the following manner. Skewer the end of one piece of courgette. Add a piece of marinated beef onto the skewer and wrap the courgette around the beef so that it cups around half the beef. Add a piece of the red onion and bring the courgette around on top of it. Keep alternating between the beef and onions and forming the courgette in an S shape around them. Fill all the skewers in the same manner.

5   30 minutes before you wish to grill the beef, light your barbeque or, if you have a gas-fired grill, pre-heat it 15 minutes before grilling.

6   Once the flames have subsided but the barbeque is still hot, cook the meat for 8 minutes, turning the skewers over 2 or 3 times during the cooking time. This will give you medium rare meat. Serve on warmed dinner plates.

For the onions:

8 medium-sized red onions — peeled and quartered

Olive oil

1 teaspoon Vincotto or a sweet vinegar, such as a balsamic (see suppliers)

Salt and pepper

1   Pour a little olive oil, Vincotto, salt and pepper into a shallow pan placed over medium heat. Add the onions in quarters and cook very slowly for 45 minutes to one hour. The onions should be very soft. Be careful as you turn them to try and keep them in quarters.

For the courgettes:

8 medium-sized green or yellow courgettes (zucchini) or a mixture of both — ends trimmed and thinly sliced lenghtwise

Olive oil

Salt and pepper

1   Pour the olive oil into a large frying pan placed over medium-high heat. Add in the sliced courgettes, a little salt and pepper and cook for 4 – 5 minutes, turning them once. They should have softened slightly. Keep warm until they are ready to be used.

Preparing the beef skewers

43

Origins

Mayonnaise has a number of possible origins. It has been said that Duc de Richelieu or his chef created the sauce after capturing the port of Mahon on the island of Minorca in 1756, and named it Mahonnaise. But other historians contest that theory and say it comes from The Duke of Mayenne in 1589 who took the time to finish his lunch of chicken with cold sauce before he went into battle, and thus the sauce was named after him! Either way the sauce is an emulsion of egg yolks and oil.

For the tomatoes:

16 small to medium tomatoes — preferably different varieties — cut in half

8 long rosemary stems — left intact

Coarse salt

Fresh pepper

1 Carefully thread four tomato halves onto each of the rosemary stems. The easiest way to do this is by pushing the skin side of the tomato through the twig-like end of the rosemary. Place all the rosemary skewers onto a plate and add a little salt and pepper to each one.

2 Grill these on the side of the barbecue where the temperature is less hot. They will need to cook for 5 – 6 minutes, turning them once or twice. Serve alongside the marinated beef and with the herb mayonnaise.

THE KEY:

To create fool-proof mayonnaise you have to be careful not to add the oil in too quickly otherwise this will cause the sauce to separate. Also make sure that all the ingredients are at room temperature — even the egg yolk, as this will help the sauce to bind quickly.

For the herb mayonnaise:

1 egg yolk

2 tablespoons Dijon mustard

2 tablespoons vegetable oil

Olive oil

Juice of 1 lemon

1 bunch flat leaf parsley (1 cup) — finely chopped

8 – 10 sprigs de-stemmed (1/2 cup) fresh oregano — finely chopped

1 small bunch fresh cilantro — finely chopped

Salt and pepper

1 Put the egg yolk, mustard and lemon juice into a blender. With the motor running on the lowest speed, very slowly add the vegetable oil in a teaspoon at a time. You should have a very thick mixture.

2 Once the vegetable oil has been completely mixed in with the mustard, slowly drizzle in the olive oil, always with the motor running, but now at a faster speed. You will need at least a 1/2 cup of olive oil. Once the mayonnaise is nice and thick you can add in all the herbs, some salt and pepper. If you like your mayonnaise a little sharp, then add in a little more lemon juice.

3 Serve a large spoonful of this alongside the grilled beef and vegetables.

NOTE: If it is a hot day, refrigerate the mayonnaise until ready to serve.

Origins

Mint, the common name of most plants from the genus *menthe*, it has been cultivated for millennia. It was brought to England by the Romans who used to, amongst other things, pickle it in vinegar. Its medicinal and culinary uses are spread through centuries of cookbooks and it features strongly in English and Middle Eastern food. In Greek mythology it is said that Prosperina, consort of the god Pluto, grew jealous of his attentions to the nymph Mintha and turned her into the plant — hence its name.

SUMMER 'FOOL' WITH MINT CREAM

This is a delightful, fresh and easy summer dessert to make. It is perfect for a summer barbeque or afternoon tea.

Serves 8 people

For the purée:

2 mangoes — peeled and cut into large pieces

3 peaches — peeled and cut into quarters

Zest and juice of 1 orange

For the cream:

1 large bunch mint — leaves removed from stems and finely chopped

1 pint whipping cream

1 tablespoon sugar

For the fruit:

1 basket raspberries

2 baskets blueberries

2 tablespoons light brown sugar

1 tablespoon butter

Juice of 1/2 lemon

1   Place the mangoes, peaches, orange zest and juice in a blender. Run the motor until you have a fine purée. You may need to scrape down the sides once or twice to make sure all the pieces are puréed. Pour the purée into the bottom of a large, pretty glass serving bowl. Cover and refrigerate.

2   Pour the cream, sugar and mint into a blender and run the motor so that the cream takes on a slightly green tinge. This will take about 60 seconds. Then pour the cream into a bowl and using a hand-held mixer, beat the cream until stiff peaks are formed. Cover and refrigerate until you are ready to assemble the Fool.

3   Place a piece of foil on a counter that is approximately 16 inches long. Place all the berries in the center of the foil. Sprinkle with the sugar, lemon juice and dot with the butter. Close the foil up around the fruit, creating a pouch, ensuring that it is completely sealed.

4   Place the sealed pouch over the embers of the grill for 10 minutes. If you don't have a grill, place all the fruit ingredients in a medium-sized skillet and cook over medium heat for 5 minutes. The fruit should be slightly syrupy but not completely cooked. Let cool for 5 – 10 minutes.

5   To assemble the fool, remove the bowl with the purée from the refrigerator. Carefully pour the partially-cooked fruit over the purée and then top the fruit with the mint cream. You can decorate the surface of the fool with additional berries if you like.

Leek Napoleon with Lemon and Chive Vinaigrette
Grilled Fish with Herbes de Poisson and Green Onions
Ratatouille
Hot Lemon Soufflés with Raspberry Sauce

COOKING SCHEDULE

Starting 2 hours before you plan to eat your first course:

- Make the Leek Napoleon and refrigerate.

- Make the base for the soufflés through step 4 of the recipe.

- Make the ratatouille and keep warm once finished.

- Prepare the fish for the grill.

- Light the grill if you have a charcoal version.

- Place fish on grill just before you sit down to eat first course.

- If you are planning on serving individual soufflés, put them in the oven at the beginning of the main course as they only need 20 minutes to cook. If you are making a large soufflé it will need 35 – 40 minutes to cook and will need to be put in the oven as you sit down to eat the first course.

LEEK NAPOLEON WITH A LEMON AND CHIVE VINAIGRETTE

Serves 8 people

12 Leeks — outer leaves pulled off and ends trimmed, you should have a piece that is about 10 inches long

8 oz cream cheese

5 oz goat cheese

Zest of 1 large lemon

1 tablespoon lemon juice

2 tablespoons finely chopped chives

Freshly ground black pepper

2 oz mache salad greens (lamb's lettuce)

1 Carefully wash the trimmed ends of the leeks to remove any dirt that may be between the leaves. Place the leeks in a vegetable steamer and cook until just tender. This should take about 8 minutes. Remove from the strainer and set aside to cool. Drain any water from the leeks.

2 Place all the remaining ingredients except the salad greens in a food processor and pulse until smooth. You may need to add a little more lemon juice if the mixture seems too stiff.

3 Line a terrine mold with plastic wrap; leaving enough wrap hanging over the sides (you will need this when you wrap up the napoleon at the end).

4 Place 4 leeks in the bottom of the mold with all the white ends together. Cover the leeks with a third of the goat cheese mixture, spreading it out in an even layer. Place another 4 leeks on top of the cream mixture, making sure that the white ends are at the opposite end of the terrine. Cover with another third of the goat cheese mixture. Place the final

four leeks on top, reversing the direction of the leeks once again. Cover with the remaining goat cheese mixture.

5 Fold the plastic wrap over the top of the napoleon, making sure that it is completely covered. Place an object, such as a bag of dried beans, on top of the napoleon. Refrigerate until it is time to serve. It needs at least 2 hours in the refrigerator.

6 To serve the napoleon: Remove the terrine from the refrigerator and invert it onto a wooden cutting board. Peel off the plastic wrap. Using a very sharp knife, carefully slice 3/4-inch thick slices and place each slice in the center of a salad plate. Place a few leaves of mache next to the napoleon and drizzle some of the vinaigrette (see recipe below) around the side of the leeks.

For the vinaigrette:

1 1/2 tablespoons white balsamic vinegar

3 tablespoons lemon olive oil or very good fruity virgin olive oil

1 teaspoon mustard

1 teaspoon mayonnaise

1 teaspoon lemon zest

1 tablespoon chopped chives

Large pinch Sel de Mer

Freshly-ground black peppercorns

1 Place all the ingredients in a small bowl and whisk well together. Serve alongside leeks.

Origins

The Egyptians, Greeks and Romans all cultivated leeks throughout their long histories. Emperor Nero is said to have consumed them daily believing that their properties would improve his singing voice. He earned the name *porropphagus* or *leek-eater* as a result. Leeks come from the onion family, although they are milder and sweeter in flavor than regular onions. Called *porrum* in Latin, from where the French get the word *poirreau*, the English arrived at the name leek from the Anglo-Saxon word *leac*.

GRILLED FISH WITH HERBES DE POISSON AND GREEN ONIONS

This is a simple, delicious way of grilling fish and ensures that the fish stays moist. You can cook this with either a whole fish or filets of fish. This dish works well with a fish-shaped wire barbeque frame or basket that you place on top of the grill. I have given an alternative method if you do not have a frame.

Serves 8 people

1 whole fish (3lbs) — gutted, head and tail left on or 2 lbs of fish filets — choose a firm white fish

1 tablespoon of the following mixture — coarse sea salt, mustard seeds, dried fennel seeds and dried coriander — or 1 tablespoon Herbes de Poisson (see suppliers)

2 tablespoons lemon olive oil

1/2 bunch dill

2 bunches green onions — rinsed under cold water but not dried, ends trimmed

1   Light your grill 30 minutes prior to cooking the fish or pre-heat your gas-fired grill.

2   In a small bowl combine the olive oil and herb/salt mixture and stir to combine well.

3   Place the fish in a shallow pan or dish and drizzle the olive oil mixture over the fish. Use your fingers to cover the fish well with the herb mixture.

4   If you are using a fish-shaped frame, line the bottom half of the frame with half of the green onions and half of the dill. Place the fish or filets of fish on top of the bed of green onions and dill and then cover the fish with the remaining dill and green onions. Close the top of the wire frame.

5   Place the wire frame containing the fish directly on the grill. Cook for 7 – 8 minutes and then turn the frame over to cook the fish on the other side for another 7 minutes. Remove from the grill and serve on hot plates with the ratatouille. Remember to serve some of the char-grilled green onions on each plate.

Alternative method:

1   Follow the directions up to step 3 above. Take a large piece of foil and set it shiny side up. Place half the green onions and half the dill in the middle of the foil, covering an area that is the same size as the fish. Place the fish on top of the green onions. Place the remaining dill and green onions on top of the fish.

2   Enclose the fish completely with the foil and then place the foil pouch over the hot coals and grill for 7 – 8 minutes. Using oven gloves, very carefully turn the pouch over and continue to cook on the other side for another 5 minutes. Carefully remove the pouch from the barbeque and set on a large plate. Be equally careful when you open the pouch as it will release steam.

3   Serve on hot plates with the ratatouille.

RATATOUILLE

4 – 5 medium yellow onions — cut in half and then thinly sliced

1 large or 2 medium aubergines (eggplant) — thinly sliced and cut into small cubes

4 – 6 courgettes (zucchini) — cut into quarters lengthwise and then into small cubes

8 – 10 medium tomatoes — Romas work well — quartered and diced

3 cloves garlic — either finely chopped or crushed

Olive oil

Salt and pepper

1 bay leaf

1 Pour a little olive oil in a large heavy-bottomed saucepan placed over medium-high heat. Add the chopped onions. Cook until soft and lightly browned, about 10 minutes.

2 Whilst the onions are browning, pour a little olive oil into a large frying pan or heavy skillet placed over medium-high heat, and sauté the chopped aubergines until lightly browned. Approximately 8 – 10 minutes. Once cooked add the aubergines to the onions. Add salt and pepper to taste.

3 In the same frying pan/ skillet pour a little more olive oil and add the courgettes. Cook until lightly browned — approximately 5 – 7 minutes. Once cooked add these to the onion mixture.

4 In the same frying pan / skillet add a touch more olive oil and cook the tomatoes over high heat with the garlic for 2 – 3 minutes — letting any excess water from the tomatoes evaporate. Add the tomatoes to the onion mixture.

5 Cook all the vegetables together with the bay leaf for a further 30 – 45 minutes. Add salt and pepper to your liking. Remove the bay leaf just before serving. It is also excellent served cold the next day.

NOTES: Ratatouille is traditionally made with the addition of red and green peppers. They are thinly sliced and also cooked separately before adding to the onion mixture — usually after the courgettes but before the tomatoes. I prefer to make it without the peppers when serving it with fish. There are many recipes for cooking Ratatouille, each varying in the order that one cooks the vegetables. Purists insist that each vegetable is cooked separately before being mixed in with the onions as this seals in the taste of each vegetable. *One last note:* Do not cover your Ratatouille as this will cause too much moisture in the dish.

THE KEY:

Soufflés have a reputation for being difficult, but really only two things need to happen to ensure success and the accompanying 'oohs' and 'aahs' of one's guests. Firstly, do not over beat the egg whites. They should be firm but not too stiff. Secondly, be sure to incorporate the egg whites slowly into the base.

Opening the oven door to check on the soufflé will not, contrary to popular belief, cause the soufflé to fall as the temperature will remain fairly steady for the 30 seconds it takes to peek at it. A large drop in temperature will cause it to fall, which is why, when you take the soufflé out of the oven, it needs to be served as quickly as possible.

HOT LEMON SOUFFLÉS WITH RASPBERRY SAUCE

My love of Pots de Crème is closely followed by the passion I have for soufflés. I make them in a variety of guises, usually savory. One of our favorite meals at home is a cheese soufflé with a large green salad. This sweet one came about in one of my lemon phases!

Serves 8 people

2 1/2 oz (5 tablespoons) butter plus
   2 tablespoons for the ramekins or
   soufflé mold

5 tablespoons unbleached flour

1 1/4 cups milk

8 oz (1 cup less 1 tablespoon) sugar,
   plus additional sugar to coat each
   of the ramekins

2 tablespoons crème fraiche

Juice of 1 1/2 lemons

Zest of 3 lemons

4 egg yolks

7 egg whites

1   Preheat the oven to 400 degrees.

2   Use the 2 tablespoons of butter to grease the inside of the ramekins or one large soufflé mold — you may need a little less if you a using one large mold. Spoon a little sugar into each ramekin or the large mold and tilt it around so that the sugar covers the inside of the ramekins.

3   Melt the butter in a large saucepan placed over medium heat. When the butter has completely melted, add in the flour and stir until it has completely absorbed the butter and thickens into a paste. Add in the milk and continue stirring until you have a thick, creamy mixture. Stir in the sugar and cook for a further 2 minutes. Remove from the heat.

4   Add in the crème fraiche, lemon zest and lemon juice, stirring well to combine all the ingredients. Making sure that

the mixture is not too hot, whisk in the egg yolks so that you have a smooth, homogenous mixture. Set aside.

5   Beat the egg whites until they are just firm. You don't want to over beat them as this will create a dry soufflé. Gently fold the egg whites into the soufflé base until they are completely incorporated. You should have no pockets of just egg white mixture. The texture should be quite stiff. Spoon or pour the soufflé mixture into each of the ramekins or the large mold.

6   Bake for 20 – 25 minutes for the individual ones or 40 minutes for the large one. Serve immediately.

NOTE: You can make the soufflé mixture up to 2 hours ahead of time and keep refrigerated in its mold until ready to bake.

RASPBERRY SAUCE

Serves 8 as an accompaniment to the soufflé

1 lb raspberries

Zest and juice of 1/2 orange

2 teaspoons crème de cassis (optional)

1   Place the raspberries, orange zest, orange juice and crème de cassis (if you are using it) in a blender and purée until smooth. Keep chilled until ready to serve. If you wish to have a smooth sauce, strain it through a medium-sized mesh strainer into a small bowl. Note though that you will not have as much volume this way.

Origins

Soufflé is the French word for breath. In culinary terms, the word refers to a light, ethereal dish just stiff enough to hold its shape, and which may be savory or sweet, hot or cold. The stiffly-beaten egg whites add air into the base custard which is created by making a *roux* and adding milk. This is the basis of a *béchamel* sauce (white sauce). Incorporating the egg whites into this sauce is credited to Antoine Beauvillers, a chef who founded what is considered to be the first 'real' restaurant in Paris, called *La Grande Taverne de Londres* in 1782. Recipes for his Soufflé appear in his renowned 1814 cookbook *L'Art de Cuisinier*.

Cucumber and Avocado Soup with Tomato 'Tartare'
Summer Vegetable Terrine with Tomato-Lemon Sauce
Blueberry Crumbles with Lemon Devon Cream

COOKING SCHEDULE

This is a meal where the main course should be made a day ahead or in the morning if it is being served in the evening.

- Make the Summer Vegetable Terrine from start to finish. It will need time to set — at least 8 hours. It takes about 1 to 1 ½ hours to make the dish.

- Make the soup. It needs a minimum of 30 minutes to chill. It can be made up to 1 ½ hours before serving, but only takes about 10 – 15 minutes to prepare from start to finish.

- Make the Tomato 'Tartare'.

- Make the tomato-lemon sauce and set aside.

- Prepare blueberry crumble — put in oven as you serve the first course.

CUCUMBER AND AVOCADO SOUP WITH A TOMATO 'TARTARE'

This chilled soup is perfect for a hot summer's day. The tomato 'tartare' is delicious with the silky smooth texture of the soup.

Serves 8 people

1 ½ English cucumbers — peeled and coarsely chopped

2 – 3 ripe avocadoes (preferably Hass) — cut in half and the flesh scooped out

2 tablespoons olive oil

Juice of 1 lemon

1 bunch chives — finely chopped (keep 1 tablespoon set aside for garnish)

1/2 bunch cilantro — finely chopped

2 teaspoons coarse grey moist sea salt

For the tomato 'tartare':

2 medium red, green or yellow heirloom tomatoes — diced into small cubes

1 teaspoon olive oil

Zest of 1 lemon

Chives — see list above

Grey sea salt

Freshly ground pepper

1/2 cup crème fraiche or thick Greek-style yogurt

1   Place the cucumber in a blender and purée until smooth. Add in the avocado and purée for just a few seconds. Add in the olive oil and the remaining ingredients and purée again for a few seconds more. You should have a very smooth, pale green soup. Refrigerate until ready to serve.

2   Combine all the 'tartare' ingredients, except the crème fraiche in a small bowl and toss to combine well.

3   To serve, divide the soup equally between eight small soup bowls. Carefully spoon a little crème fraiche (or yogurt) into the center of each bowl of soup. Add a tablespoon of the tomato 'tartare' on top of the crème fraiche (or yogurt).

Origins

The name *Persea Americana* or avocado pear has an unusual origin. The name comes from the Aztec word *ahuacatl* which means testicle.
It is unlike any other fruit having a very rich butter-like flesh and single large stone. Of all fruits, the avocado is highest in protein and oil content.
The avocado tree, a member of the laurel family, first grew in subtropical America and has been cultivated for over 7,000 years. One of the
best known avocado dishes, guacamole, is also one of the oldest. It dates to pre-Columbian times.

SUMMER VEGETABLE TERRINE WITH TOMATO-LEMON SAUCE

This is a labor of love but worth the effort as it is spectacular! It captures all the great flavors that come from a summer vegetable garden. You will be able to taste each one individually, and the combination is just delicious.

Serves 6 – 8 people

2 medium aubergines (eggplants) — ends trimmed and then cut lengthwise in 3/4-inch thick slices

6 courgettes (zucchini) — try to use 3 yellow and 3 green ones — ends trimmed and cut lengthwise into 1/2-inch thick slices

Olive oil

1 bunch green asparagus — trimmed into 2 1/2-inch pieces or the width of your terrine

1 bunch white asparagus — trimmed into 2 1/2-inch pieces or the width of your terrine (if you cannot find white asparagus, double the green asparagus)

Salt and pepper

10 large shallots — peeled and thinly sliced

8 garlic cloves — peeled and diced

1 tablespoon Herbes de Provence

1/2 teaspoon sugar

1 bunch spring onions — trimmed into 2 ^{1}/2-inch pieces or the width of your terrine

12 whole medium wild mushrooms — cleaned

Juice of 1/2 lemon

3 tomatoes — must be ripe — peeled, seeded and cut in half

1 bunch chopped chives

Students enjoying dinner at one of my cooking classes.

1   Preheat the oven to 375 degrees.

2   Place all the aubergines and courgette slices onto oiled baking pans, making sure that they are well coated. Sprinkle with salt and pepper and bake in the oven for 35 minutes. Turn the pieces from time to time, making sure that the pieces remain intact. Remove from the oven and let cool.

3   Cook the green asparagus for 5 minutes in boiling salted water until just tender and still bright green. Drain and set aside.

4   Cook the white asparagus in boiling salted water for 8 – 10 minutes until tender. Drain and set aside.

5   Put the shallots, spring onions, garlic, 2 tablespoons of olive oil, a good pinch of salt, sugar, the Herbes de Provence and a 1/4 cup of water in a heavy-bottomed skillet. Bring to a boil and cook, covered, until the shallots are half cooked — about 5 minutes. Uncover the skillet and continue cooking, stirring frequently until the shallots and garlic cloves are tender and lightly glazed. Remove from the pan and set aside.

6   Put the mushrooms in the same skillet. Add the lemon juice and some salt and cook over high heat until the mushrooms are just cooked. They should be lightly browned and just beginning to render their juice. Remove from the pan and set aside.

7   Line a 2-quart terrine with plastic wrap in which you poke a few holes with the tip of a knife. The plastic wrap should hang over the sides of the terrine.

8   Four of the aubergine slices (the outer slices) will have large, skin-covered surfaces. Put 2 of these on the bottom of the terrine, skin down, cutting them to fit if necessary. The other 2 will be used for the top. Layer half the remaining aubergine over those bottom slices.

9 Spread half the courgette slices over the aubergine (if using the two different courgette use half of each color) and cover with half the tomatoes. Cover the tomatoes with all of the garlic, spring onion and shallot mixture.

10 Cover the shallot mixture with the green asparagus by placing the pieces across the terrine (i.e., the pieces are as wide as the terrine). Spread the remaining tomatoes over the asparagus. Add all the mushrooms on top of the tomatoes and then place the white asparagus over the mushrooms.

11 Place the remaining courgette slices over the white asparagus and then the remaining aubergine over the courgette, ending with the 2 reserved outer pieces of aubergine, cutting them to fit if necessary, skin-side up.

12 Cover the terrine with parchment paper or with plastic wrap and then set a second terrine on top or use heavy weights to compress the vegetables. Refrigerate 8 hours or overnight.

13 Just before serving, unmold the terrine by inverting it onto a cutting board. Cut it with a sharp knife into 3/4-inch thick slices. Place a slice on a salad plate and serve with the tomato-lemon sauce that follows:

For the tomato-lemon sauce:

2 large ripe tomatoes — peeled and quartered

Zest and juice of 1 large lemon

2 teaspoons lemon olive oil

Large pinch of coarse sea salt

Freshly ground black pepper

1 bunch fresh chives — finely minced

1 Place all the ingredients except for the chives in a blender and purée until you have a frothy, smooth sauce.

2 Spoon a little of the sauce around the terrine slices and sprinkle the sauce with the chopped chives.

THE KEY:

The following table shows the order you assemble the terrine.

BOTTOM of terrine

1/2 aubergine slices (step 8)

1/2 courgette slices (step 9)

1/2 tomatoes (step 9)

All of the garlic-shallot mixture (step 9)

All of the green asparagus (step 10)

Remaining tomatoes (step 10)

All the mushrooms (step 10)

All white asparagus (step 10)

Remaining courgette slices (step 11)

Remaining aubergine slices (step 11)

TOP of terrine

Origins

Blueberries are native to Asia and North America. One of Earth's oldest plants, it is now widely cultivated and also harvested in the wild. Blueberries belong to the *Ericaceae* (heather) family and are renowned for their anti-oxidant properties. They are also very rich in vitamins A and C. They have formed an integral part of the Native American diet for centuries. They were used dried in puddings and cakes and as a ground spice in meats and soups.

BLUEBERRY CRUMBLES WITH LEMON DEVON CREAM

Growing up in England, we ate apple crumbles all winter long. This is a zesty summer version and the Lemon-Devon Cream is heavenly with it.

Serves 8 people

For the blueberries:

4 baskets blueberries

Chopped zest and juice of 1 lemon

2 tablespoons sugar

For the crumble:

10 oz unbleached all-purpose flour

9 oz butter — cut into little pieces

1/3 cup sugar

Cinnamon

For the Devon Cream:

6 oz Devon cream

Zest of 1 lemon

1 teaspoon cinnamon

Pinch allspice

1　Preheat the oven to 400 degrees.

2　Combine the blueberries, lemon zest, sugar and lemon juice in a large bowl. Divide the blueberries equally amongst 8 individual ramekins. Set aside.

3　To make the crumble, place all the flour in a large bowl. Add 8 oz of the butter and mix it with the flour, using the tips of your fingers, until it resembles coarse breadcrumbs. Don't worry if you have little lumps of butter left — it should look like that! Add in the sugar and mix to combine.

4　Cover the blueberries with the crumble mixture. Sprinkle a little extra cinnamon and sugar over the crumble. Dot the surface with the remaining butter. Bake in the center of the oven for 20 minutes or until golden brown.

5　Combine all the ingredients for the Devon cream until smooth and well incorporated. Serve the lemon Devon cream with the hot blueberry crumbles.

Cured Salmon with Mesclun Salad
Poached Fish with Leek and Saffron Coulis
Steven's Fingerling Potatoes
Fresh Berry Tart with Lemon Ginger Cream

COOKING SCHEDULE

Starting 2 hours before you plan to eat your first course:

- Make the tart dough and blind bake the shell.
- Prepare the cured salmon and set aside.
- Make cream for tart shell.
- Prepare the poaching stock for the fish.
- Make the saffron coulis.
- Prepare fish but do not cook it yet.
- Steam the fingerling potatoes.
- Make Mesclun Salad — toss just before serving.
- Place fish in poacher as you serve first course — it only takes 15 minutes to cook.
- Finish potatoes between first and main course.
- Serve the main course on hot plates.
- Assemble the tart just before serving — this takes 3 minutes.

CURED SALMON WITH MESCLUN SALAD

This is an excellent dish for a dinner party. Inspired by Scandinavian Gravlax, this version is quick and easy to prepare.

Serves 8 people

For the salmon:

1 lb smoked wild salmon

1 bunch chives — very finely chopped

2 tablespoons dill — very finely chopped

Zest of one lemon

1 tablespoon lemon juice

1 tablespoon lemon olive oil

1   Cover the center of 8 salad plates with slices of smoked salmon. Set aside.

2   In a small bowl mix together all the remaining ingredients. Spoon a little of the mixture over the salmon covering it evenly. Set aside for 30 minutes.

For the mesclun salad:

1 small shallot — peeled and very finely diced

3 tablespoons olive oil

2 teaspoons vinegar

1 teaspoon mustard

8 oz mesclun salad greens

1 tablespoon basil — finely shredded

1   In the bottom of a medium-sized salad bowl, mix together the shallot, olive oil, vinegar and mustard so that you have a smooth homogenous vinaigrette. Place serving utensils over the vinaigrette and then place the salad greens and basil over the utensils.

2   When you are ready to serve the salad, remove the utensils and toss the salad well. Place a little of the salad in the center of each plate on top of the salmon. Serve at room temperature.

Poached Fish with Leek and Saffron Coulis

Serves 8 people

For the poaching liquid:

Fronds of 2 fennel bulbs — roughly chopped

1 leek — cleaned and halved and cut in two

4 – 5 cardamom pods

2 teaspoons salt

1 Place all the ingredients in a fish poacher and cover with cold water. Bring to a simmer and cook for 20 minutes. Turn off the heat and leave the poaching liquid in the poacher. When the liquid has cooled a little, remove all of the vegetables from the liquid and discard them.

For the fish:

2 – 2 1/2 lbs filet of firm fish, such as bluenose sea bass or a type of snapper — you can also use a whole fish such as a pink trout or rainbow trout.

1 Place 8 dinner plates in a lightly warmed oven or in a sink full of very hot water.

2 Place the filet(s) on the rack that fits inside the fish poacher. Lower the fish into the liquid. Bring to a simmer and cook for 15 minutes.

3 Remove the fish from the poaching liquid and divide evenly amongst the warmed dinner plates. Serve with the leek and saffron coulis (see recipe below).

For the leek and saffron coulis:

1 lb leeks — halved lengthwise and washed thoroughly, green parts trimmed away, then finely sliced

5 large shallots — peeled and finely sliced

1 tablespoon butter

2 tablespoons olive oil

2 1/2 cups vegetable stock (if you have excess poaching liquid from the fish you can use that)

1 large pinch saffron

1 cup cream

2 tablespoons chives — finely chopped

Salt and pepper

1 Put the butter and olive oil in a large pan placed over medium heat. Add the sliced leeks and shallots and cook slowly for 10 minutes. You do not want the vegetables to brown, but rather to soften. Add the stock and saffron and cook for a further 10 minutes.

2 Add the cream and simmer for a further 5 minutes.

3 Pour the mixture into a blender (or purée with an immersion blender) and purée for 2 minutes or until it is completely smooth. Strain the mixture through a sieve and season with salt and pepper.

4 Keep the coulis warm until it is ready to serve. Stir in the chives at the very end.

NOTE: The plates look very pretty if you pour some of the coulis in the center of the plate, and then place the fish on top of the coulis.

Origins

Saffron, the world's most expensive spice, is obtained from the stigmas of crocus flowers. Over 70,000 flowers are needed to obtain 1lb of dried saffron, and all of them have to be picked by hand. Originally from Persia, saffron has been used medicinally, in cooking and as a dye for centuries. The world's best saffron now comes from Spain.

STEVEN'S FINGERLING POTATOES

My husband, Steven, is known amongst our friends as the master sauce maker and the potato king. He has, true to his Anglo-Saxon roots, a penchant for all things related to potatoes. His mashed potatoes are legendary and ethereal. These potatoes, whilst not fluffy, are delicious and simple to make.

Serves 8 people

1 ½ lbs fingerling potatoes — washed

2 tablespoons olive oil

1 small bunch chives — finely chopped

Zest of 1 lemon

Coarse sea salt

Freshly ground pepper

1 Place the potatoes in a large saucepan of boiling, salted water and cook until just tender — approximately 8 – 10 minutes depending on their size.

2 Drain the potatoes and return to the same pan. Add in the olive oil, chives, lemon zest and cook for 2 – 3 minutes over medium-high heat, so that the potatoes are lightly browned. Sprinkle with the coarse sea salt and add some freshly ground pepper. Serve alongside the fish.

Fresh Berry Tart with Lemon Ginger Cream

Serves 8 – 10 people

For the dough:

9 oz flour

5 1/2 oz butter

1 egg

Zest of 2 lemons

1 tablespoon sugar

1 large pinch salt

1   Preheat the oven to 375 degrees.

2   Place all of the dough ingredients into a food processor and, using repeated pulses, pulse until the dough forms into a ball. Wrap the dough in plastic wrap and refrigerate for 20 minutes.

3   Roll the dough out onto a lightly floured board so that it is 1/4 – 1/3-inch thick. Butter a 9-inch fluted tart mold with a removable bottom. Line the mold with the dough, trimming away any excess along the edges.

4   Cover the tart dough with some parchment paper and place some pie weights or dried beans on top of the paper. Blind bake (i.e., cook without filling) the tart for 20 minutes so that it is just golden brown. Remove the paper and weights and cook for a further 5 minutes. The tart shell should be golden. Remove and leave to cool to room temperature.

For the berries:

4 baskets of mixed seasonal berries, including but not limited to, raspberries, blueberries, blackberries, strawberries, red currents.

4 mint leaves — finely chopped

For the filling:

3 egg yolks

2 oz sugar (1/4 cup)

2 tablespoons flour

1 cup milk

1 vanilla pod — split

Zest of 1 lemon

1 tablespoon crystallized ginger — finely chopped

1   Place the egg yolks and one third of the sugar in a bowl and whisk until they are pale and form a light ribbon. Sift in the flour and mix well.

2   Combine the milk, remaining sugar and the split vanilla pod in a saucepan and bring to a boil. As soon as the mixture bubbles, pour about one third of the milk into the egg mixture stirring all the time. Then pour the entire egg mixture back into the remaining milk mixture and cook over low heat, stirring continuously.

3   Add in the lemon zest and ginger and cook for a further two minutes over medium-high heat. The mixture should be thick, silky and smooth. Pour the mixture into a bowl, dot with a little butter to prevent a skin from forming. Set aside. If it is a warm day, cover and refrigerate.

4   When you are ready to serve the tart, pour the cream mixture into the prebaked tart shell and, using a spatula or the back side of a spoon, cover the entire base of the tart with the cream. Cover the cream entirely with the berries and top with the chopped mint.

The Cheese Course

One of my great pleasures in the summer is a lunch made up of a large salad and a sampling of delicious fresh goat cheese and bread from the local markets. The delights of cheese can truly complement a meal. There is an expression in France, *'Jamais un bon repas sans fromage,'* which literally means, 'never a good meal without cheese.' It is a proverb we adhere to with delight in our home.

Cheese has been made for millennia. Early cheeses resembled simple concentrated curds, similar to brine-cured feta. Cheese was also the subject of one of the earliest books on a single food topic. Named *Summa Lacticintarrum*, it was printed in 1477, although written references to cheeses date back to pre-Roman times.

Cheese is made from a variety of milks. Sheep, cow, goat and water-buffalo are the most common varieties, although cheese can also be made from yak, reindeer or camel milk. Cheese features widely in France's culinary history and the country now has more than 450 officially-recognized cheeses. There are probably more, given the plethora of local, artisan cheese-makers strewn across the French countryside.

The cheese course in France always follows the main course. In England, cheese was and is served after dessert. It can also be served very successfully with a glass of Champagne as an hors d'oeuvre. One should beware not to serve too many or your guests may not enjoy the meal you have just prepared. But whatever your personal preference, here are some general guidelines to consider when putting together a cheese course.

1   Decide on the type of cheese course you wish to serve. You could focus on one type of cheese with a number of varieties. For example, assemble an all-goat cheese platter or focus on a region (Champagne, Sicily, Provence) or a country (France, Italy, Spain).

2   Create a balance of tastes and textures, from mild to strong, from soft to hard. Even when presenting a platter made up of one type of cheese you will find that its myriad varieties will give you that balance.

3   Bring your cheeses out an hour before serving them so that they are at room temperature. The flavor of cheese is muted when it is cold. However, avoid leaving them out too long, particularly if it is a warm day, as they may start to sweat.

4   Present the cheeses on a wooden board, large plate or wooden tray. You can line the tray with leaves for decorative purposes. Leave enough space around each cheese so that they do not touch each other and provide one small knife for each type of cheese.

5   Traditionally, cheese boards are made up of an odd number of cheeses as this is deemed to be more pleasing to the eye. If, however, you come across a sixth cheese that you absolutely must have, then by all means include it.

6   Serve with good fresh bread or crackers. Don't choose a bread or cracker with really strong flavors (however good) as this will detract from the cheese. You can also include nuts, dried fruit, fruit cakes — such as a fig cake — and fresh fruit such as apples, pears and grapes on your board.

7   Wine pairings are often a challenge for cheeses. There are some great combinations — Stilton with Port, Roquefort with a Sauternes, Brillat-Savarin with Champagne. Certain cheeses can make a modest wine taste much better than it actually is; conversely, you need to take care that your delicious strong cheese doesn't

These are a few of my favorite cheese board combinations:

*   All goat, with a Selles-Sur-Cher, Humboldt Fog, Chabichou, Le Chevrot and a Crottin (all pictured)

*   A Spanish selection with Manchego, Mahon, Garrotxa, Queso de Valdeon and Monte Enebro

*   A combination cheese board — different countries and a mixture of goat, cow and sheep's milk — with a Mt.Tam, St.Marcellin, Ossau-Iraty, Piave and a Stilton

kill the subtle qualities of that fabulous bottle of red wine you have carefully saved for a special occasion. The following offers a broad guideline for types of cheese and wine.

- With fresh cheeses such as goat or feta, choose a Sauvignon Blanc or a Pinot Noir. Goat cheese is also excellent with a Sancerre or Pouilly-Fumé.

- With soft cheeses and full fat cheeses such as a Vacherin, Explorateur or a Brie de Meaux, serve a Brut Champagne or a Chablis.

- With a blue cheese such as a mild gorgonzola, a Danish blue or Bleu de Bresse, a Barolo or Zinfandel would work well. The classic combinations for

Stilton and Roquefort are mentioned above. You can also serve a fruity white wine such as a Viognier.

- With mild to aged cheddars, aged parmesans, Machego, Beaufort and other hard cheeses, good hearty red wines are a great paring. You could also include a Reblochon or Pont L'Eveque in this group as long as they are not over-ripe.

8   After you have served your cheeses, wrap each cheese up separately in waxed paper if you can. Alternatively, you can use parchment paper, foil or ziploc bags. Try to avoid plastic wrap as it tends to suffocate the cheese. Although cheeses are ideally kept in a cool room, keeping them in a separate drawer in your refrigerator will also work well.

SUPPLIERS/SOURCES

I am often asked where I buy my produce, fish, meat, flowers and wine. This list of purveyors, shops and markets are the ones I use whilst in California. They have all proved to be reliable, and I heartily recommend them all.

Santa Barbara:

CHEESE
C'est Cheese
www.cestcheese.com
(805) 965-0318

The best local shop for wonderful cheese and other gourmet items run by a charming couple, Kathryn and Michael Graham.

FLOWERS
Tricia Fountaine Designs
(805) 685-6481

The best floral and event design company in Santa Barbara.

HERBS AND SPICES
Montecito Country Kitchen
www.montecitocountrykitchen.com
(805) 969-1519

A great resource for exotic salts, herbs, spice blends and olive oils. This is the source for the Herbes de Poisson used in the recipe on page 50.

MEAT
Shalhoob Meat Company
(805) 963-7733

A wholesale meat company that also sells retail at its rather offbeat location on Grey Avenue. Excellent beef and duck.

PRODUCE
Santa Barbara's Farmers' markets
www.sbfarmersmarket.org
(805) 962-5354

Held almost every day of the week, showcasing the best of the organic farmers produce.

At the farmers' market, I would highly recommend the following farms:

> Fairview Gardens
> www.fairviewgardens.org
> Great local organic farm.

> Peacock Farms
> www.peacockfamilyfarms.com
> Eggs, dried fruit

> Pudwill Farms
> (805) 268-4536
> Great berries and figs

> Windrose Farms
> www.windrosefarm.org
> Fragrant heirloom tomatoes, squash and heirloom spuds

Tri-County Produce
(805) 965-4558

A great place for organic vegetables if you cannot get to the farmers' market.

SEAFOOD
Kanaloa Seafood
www.kanaloa.com
1-888-KANALOA

Located on Gutierrez Street in Santa Barbara, Kanaloa offers the best, most varied and freshest seafood available.

WINE
Lazy Acres Market (ask for Bob)
(805) 564-4410,

Tri-County Produce
(805) 965-4558

Los Angeles:

BREAD
La Brea Bakery
www.labreabakery.com
(323) 939-6813

Open since 1989, America's most widely recognized artisan bakery sells delicious loaves from its original location on South La Brea Avenue and also nationwide.

CHEESE
The Cheese Store
www.cheesestorebh com
(310) 278-2855

The best cheese shop in Southern California. Over 400 fabulous cheeses and other delicious culinary products. This shop is also the source of the Vincotto used in the recipe on page 43, the fig purée used in The Peach and Heirloom Tomato Salad on page 28 and the apple bouquet vinegar used on page 40.

PRODUCE & FLOWERS
Santa Monica's now famous Wednesday market is the largest in California and supplies many of Los Angeles' great restaurants. Worth a trip just to discover all sorts of seasonal goodies.
www.santa-monica.org/farmers_market

SEAFOOD
Santa Monica Seafood
www.santamonicaseafood.com
(310) 393-5244

A wonderful seafood store which supplies many of the top restaurants in southern California. Their retail outlet is spectacular.

CONVERSION TABLE

Here is a convenient conversion table changing those pesky pounds and ounces, pints and cups into all things metric.

Dry Measures

U.S. SYSTEM TABLESPOONS, OUNCES AND POUNDS	METRIC SYSTEM GRAMS, KILOS
1 teaspoon	0.5 grams
3 teaspoons or 1 tablespoon	14.3 grams
2 tablespoons or 1 ounce	28.4 grams
2 oz (usually 1/4 cup — see note)	56.7 grams
4 oz (usually 1/2 cup) or 1 stick butter	113.4 grams
8 oz (usually 1 cup) = 1/2 lb	226.8 grams
16 oz (usually 2 cups) = 1 lb	453.6 grams

NOTE: I strongly recommend that you use a kitchen scale. A recipe that calls for 1 cup of flour and 1 cup of sugar does not mean that you use 8 ounces of flour and 8 ounces of sugar! 1 cup of flour actually weighs just over 4 ounces and a cup of sugar weighs just over 8 ounces. A large difference, particularly in baking! Hence the reason for listing both the cup amount and the weight in my recipes.

Liquid Measures

U.S. SYSTEM TABLESPOONS, OUNCES, PINTS AND QUARTS	METRIC SYSTEM LITERS
1/4 cup liquid	59 milliliters
1/2 cup liquid	118 milliliters
1 cup liquid	237 milliliters
2 cups liquid — 1 pint	474 milliliters (just under 1/2 liter)
2 pints — 1 quart	948 milliliters (just under 1 liter)
2 pints plus a 1/4 cup	1 liter

Nearly all ovens outside America are calibrated in Celsius rather than Fahrenheit.

Oven Temperatures

FAHRENHEIT	CELSIUS
32 degrees F (freezing)	0 degrees C
100 degrees F	38 degrees C
200 degrees F (water boils at 212°F)	93 degrees C (water boils at 100°C)
300 degrees F	149 degrees C
350 degrees F	177 degrees C
400 degrees F	205 degrees C
450 degrees F	232 degrees C

index

CREATING A BOOK is always a collaborative work, and there are many people whom I would like to thank for all their help with this project.

My first thanks go to everyone at Media 27 who has done such an amazing job with the book design and production. All of you turn what could be an arduous process into a creative and enriching experience.

Particular thanks go to Judi Muller for her tireless work on the layout, beautiful design and fine attention to detail; to Ruth Verbois for dealing with the myriad of publication details; to Shukri Farhad for his negotiating and scheduling skills; to Philippe Denier for all his help with the photo shoot and to Mike Verbois for the exquisite food photos taken during our epic photo shoot. I hope you enjoyed the food! You have made the task of putting together this book a delight and seamless. Your energy and enthusiasm have been wonderful. Thank you to all of you.

To Michel Richard – Merci Michel for allowing me to spend some time in your kitchen at Citrus all those years ago and for sharing your incredible creativity with all those around you. Your have been an inspiration.

Merci, merci Ann Marie. A huge thank you from your partner in cream, for the five great years we taught together. I treasure all of those laughter-filled evenings in your beautiful home, our many, many trips, and all the delicious things, including the beautiful book we created together.

My thanks also go to Sherry Stockwell who has opened up The Masini Adobe and welcomed my

cooking school into her amazing two-hundred-year old home. It has been a delight to teach there. Thank you, too, Zita for tirelessly working during the classes and enabling everything to run smoothly.

The school, of course, could not be possible without the continued support of all my wonderful students. Thank you all for your attentiveness in the kitchen, enthusiasm around the dining room table and for your continued encouragement for this book.

As the school heads into its ninth year, I would like to thank Tony Princiotta of The Cheese Store in Beverly Hills for continuing to bring his charm and many talents to each series I teach. Merci Kathryn and Michael Graham of C'est Cheese in Santa Barbara for also sharing your knowledge of all cheese related things with my students over the last three years. These classes have been a delight.

To Celeste and Charles for letting us take pictures in and around their beautiful Santa Ynez home and letting me invade their kitchen, computer equipment and all!

To Tricia Fountaine – Your flowers make our dinner tables look

magnificent. Thank you for all of your help, creativity and encouragement.

To Nicola Ghersen – Thank you for your help with the food prep on the photo shoot.

Merci, merci to Michele Gilbert for your faultless proofreading. How can I thank you? It is an endless task. I am hugely grateful to you for your keen, precise eyes and crisp mind editing out all those extraneous commas and some of my quirky trans-Atlantic sayings.

To Peter Beale, my lovely father, for racing me around France as a young child and putting all those intoxicating food ideas into my head. Merci for all those delicious meals and your continued enthusiasm and encouragement of all my culinary and literary endeavors.

To Monique Fay, my wonderful mother, for tirelessly helping with all the cooking classes, the photo shoot, for traipsing around the countryside, through vineyards and into Celeste's garden in search of the perfect shot and for taking the great pictures of me teaching. Not being enamored of having my picture taken, I found you made the task easy and painless. Thank you for your love, enthusiasm and unwavering faith that all things are possible.

Finally, a giant thank you to Olivia, Alexandre and Steven for your unending love and belief in me. You have supported all my projects, tasted all those dishes time and again, waited patiently whilst I photographed blueberries for hours on end and smiled indulgently as I wandered off to yet another farmers' market. I could not have done this book, nor the school without you. Merci – mille fois merci.

Photographs by Monique Fay, Pascale Beale-Groom and Mike Verbois